Celebrate Martin Luther King, Jr., Day

Other titles in the *Celebrate Holidays* series

Celebrate Chinese New Year
ISBN 0-7660-2577-2

◆

Celebrate Cinco de Mayo
ISBN 0-7660-2579-9

◆

Celebrate Columbus Day
ISBN 0-7660-2580-2

◆

Celebrate Halloween
ISBN 0-7660-2491-1

◆

Celebrate Martin Luther King, Jr., Day
ISBN 0-7660-2492-X

◆

Celebrate St. Patrick's Day
ISBN 0-7660-2581-0

◆

Celebrate Thanksgiving Day
ISBN 0-7660-2578-0

CELEBRATE HOLIDAYS

Celebrate Martin Luther King, Jr., Day

Laura S. Jeffrey

Martin Luther King, Jr., gives a speech at
the March on Washington in 1963.

Enslow Publishers, Inc.
40 Industrial Road
Box 398
Berkeley Heights, NJ 07922
USA

http://www.enslow.com

Library of Congress Cataloging-in-Publication Data

Jeffrey, Laura S.
    Celebrate Martin Luther King, Jr., Day / Laura S. Jeffrey.
       p. cm. — (Celebrate holidays)
    Includes bibliographical references and index.
    ISBN-10: 0-7660-2492-X
       1. Martin Luther King, Jr., Day—Juvenile literature. 2. King, Martin Luther, Jr., 1929–1968—Juvenile literature. I. Title. II. Series.
    E185.97.K5J44 2006
    394.261—dc22

                               2005028110

    ISBN-13: 978-0-7660-2492-2

Printed in the United States of America

10 9 8 7 6 5 4 3 2

To Our Readers: We have done our best to make sure all Internet Addresses in this book were active and appropriate when we went to press. However, the author and the publisher have no control over and assume no liability for the material available on those Internet sites or on other Web sites they may link to. Any comments or suggestions can be sent by e-mail to comments@ enslow.com or to the address on the back cover.

Every effort has been made to locate all copyright holders of material used in this book. If any errors or omissions have occurred, corrections will be made in future editions of this book.

Illustration Credits: AP Photo, pp. 13, 16; AP/Wide World, pp. 3, 31; Associated Press, AP, pp. 6, 8, 25, 29, 35, 39, 43, 44 , 50, 58, 61, 64, 71, 73, 80, 83; Associated Press, Chillicothe Gazette, p. 54; Associated Press, The Daily Times, p. 66; Associated Press, Long Beach Press, p. 75; Associated Press, Montgomery Sheriffs Department, p. 21; Associated Press, Stillwater Newspress, p. 52; Corel Corporation, p. 11; © 2006 Jupiterimages, pp. 7, 17, 36, 37, 55, 67, 81, 89; Library of Congress, p. 15; Morehouse College, p. 19.

Cover Illustration: AP/Wide World.

CONTENTS

On August 28, 1963, Martin Luther King, Jr., addressed a crowd in Washington, D.C.

"... A Dream Today!"

Gene Young was twelve years old when he embarked on a road trip of almost one thousand miles and became part of United States history. It was the summer of 1963, and the Jackson, Mississippi, youth was one of approximately two hundred fifty thousand people who journeyed to the nation's capital to take part in the March on Washington, D.C., for Civil Rights.

Segregation was a big part of life in the 1950s. This sign in Louisiana told people who was allowed into that establishment.

During Gene's childhood, segregation in the United States was legal. Segregation is the policy of separating people by race. In the 1890s, after the Civil War (1861–1865), the United States Supreme Court ruled that states could have segregation laws as long as blacks and whites were offered equal facilities. This ruling became known as the "separate but equal" doctrine, or principle. But the facilities and services offered to blacks usually were not as good as those offered to whites.

Then, in 1954, the United States Supreme Court ruled that segregation in public schools was illegal. However, many Southern states resisted the ruling. Segregation remained a fact in many other aspects of society. Blacks were not allowed to eat in the same restaurants as whites. They were not allowed to shop in the same stores, or even drink from the same water fountains. Generally, blacks were considered inferior to whites and were treated unfairly.

Beginning in the mid-1950s, many American citizens began protesting the inequalities and demanding change. This period is now known as the civil rights movement. Many of the protests were led by an African-American minister named Martin Luther King, Jr.

King was the leader of the Southern Christian Leadership Conference, a civil rights group. He led boycotts and demonstrations, and spoke forcefully for change through nonviolence. He motivated many people to work peacefully for equal rights even though King himself had been harassed and arrested by authorities.

Now it was 1963, and the United States Congress was getting ready to consider a bill that would end segregation and guarantee equal rights for all citizens. This bill would not become law unless a majority of the members of the United States Congress voted to approve it.

King and other African-American leaders in the civil rights movement realized how important it was to show lawmakers that many, many American citizens supported the legislation. So they came up with a grand plan: the March on Washington. They chose August 28, 1963, as the date, and encouraged all Americans to come to the nation's capital that day in a show of support. They hired buses and trains to transport people from cities and towns all over the United States.

It was on one of these chartered buses that Gene Young came to Washington without his parents. He did not have much money with him,

This is the Lincoln Memorial in Washington, D.C. King gave his speech in front of the memorial.

but his mother had made him sandwiches and fried fish for the long bus ride.[1]

"Every mile of that trip was exciting," he recalled forty years later. "We sang freedom songs; we stopped in Atlanta to pick up more people. When we pulled into Washington . . . I couldn't believe it. I had never seen that many people, on buses, coming off trains. Black people and white people, together."[2]

Approximately a quarter of a million people had come to Washington in the largest demonstration to date. The protesters were of all ages, races, and religions. Hundreds of thousands more Americans listened to the events of the day on radios and television sets. *The New York Times* reported the next day that many people who watched or listened to the events wished that they, too, could have been there.[3]

Washington, D.C., officials were worried that the march might turn violent. Sales of liquor were outlawed for the day, and extra police officers were called to duty. But the crowd, though loud and large, was peaceful. First, they gathered at the Washington Monument, where folk singer Joan Baez and others performed. Then, the protesters linked arms and walked up Independence and Constitution avenues to the Lincoln Memorial. There, they listened as speaker after speaker called for equal rights.

King was the final speaker of the day. His speech energized the crowd.[4]

"I have a dream. . . .," King declared. "I have a dream that one day . . . sons of former slaves and

Hundreds of thousands of people of all ages, races, and religions attended the March on Washington in 1963.

sons of former slave-owners will be able to sit down together at the table of brotherhood."

". . . I have a dream my four little children will one day live in a nation where they will not be judged by the color of their skin but by the content of their character. I have a dream today!"[5]

The huge crowd roared with approval. "It will be a long time before [Washington, D.C.] forgets the melodious and melancholy voice of the Reverend Dr. Martin Luther King, Jr., crying out his dreams to the multitude," *The New York Times* reported.[6] The newspaper also said that King "touched all the themes of the day only better than anybody else. . . . He was both militant and sad, and he sent the crowd away feeling that the long journey had been worthwhile."[7]

With that speech, King became the face and voice for equality and justice. The civil rights movement was a success, and King became a hero and role model for many Americans, black and white alike. He also became a hero and role model for citizens in other countries, too.

After King's untimely death, many people sought to honor him with a holiday. Never before had an African American received such an honor. Only two other individuals, George Washington and Abraham Lincoln, had received this

The crowd extended from the Lincoln Memorial to the Washington Monument.

distinction, and they had been presidents. Who, then, was Martin Luther King, Jr.? And why was he worthy of a holiday named after him?

Martin Luther King, Jr., went to a school for only black children, like this one in South Carolina.

Leader of the Movement

Martin Luther King, Jr., was born Michael King, Jr., on January 15, 1929, in Atlanta, Georgia. He was the second child of Michael King, Sr., and his wife, Alberta. Michael King, Sr., later changed his name and his son's name to honor Martin Luther, the founder of the Lutheran church.

Martin had an older sister, Willie, and a younger brother, Alfred. Martin's father and grandfather were ministers, and the middle-class King family was generally happy. However, like most

African Americans, Martin Sr. was frustrated by the segregation he and his family were forced to live with daily. Martin Sr.'s openness about the injustice of segregation influenced young Martin and the other King children[1] Segregation is the separation of people based on their race. A United States Supreme Court ruling in 1896 made segregation legal. This ruling is known as *Plessy* v. *Ferguson.*

The ruling required separate but equal facilities for blacks and whites. But facilities for African Americans usually were inferior. Many Southern states also adopted laws that called for separate schools, drinking fountains, bathrooms, hotels, and restaurants, among other things. These laws were called Jim Crow laws. They were named after an African-American minstrel character portrayed by a white actor in the mid-nineteenth century. A minstrel is an entertainer who sings, tells jokes, and performs musical skits.

Martin attended various segregated public schools in Atlanta. In 1944, he entered Morehouse College. He was only fifteen years old. At Morehouse, Martin decided to follow his grandfather and father's career path and become a minister. Martin became an ordained Baptist minister in February 1948. A few months later, he graduated

King entered Morehouse College in 1944, when he was only fifteen years old.

from Morehouse with a bachelor's degree in sociology.

King continued his education at Crozer Theological Seminary in Chester, Pennsylvania. There, he studied the teachings of Mahatma Gandhi (1869–1948). Gandhi was a leader in the country of India who supported nonviolence to achieve social change. Gandhi worked for many years to free his country from British rule.

King graduated from Crozer in 1951 with a bachelor's degree in divinity. Next, he enrolled at

Boston University in Massachusetts. He began studies for a doctorate in theology. In 1952, King met Coretta Scott. She was a student studying music at a nearby college. The couple began dating. They were married in June 1953 and lived in Boston while working on their degrees. In 1954 they moved to Montgomery, Alabama, where King became pastor of the Dexter Avenue Baptist Church. He was awarded his doctorate in 1955.

In 1954, the United States Supreme Court made a very important ruling. In *Brown* v. *Board of Education of Topeka*, the nation's highest court ruled that "separate educational facilities are . . . unequal."[2] Public schools were ordered to integrate immediately.

Despite this ruling, many Southern states continued to send black and white children to separate schools. They also kept the Jim Crow laws.

In November 1955, Coretta Scott King gave birth to a baby girl. The Kings named her Yolanda. She was the first of the couple's four children. A month after the baby was born, an event sparked the beginning of what became known as the civil rights movement.

On December 1, 1955, Rosa Parks rode a Montgomery city bus home from her job as

A Montgomery, Alabama, Sheriff's Department booking photo of Rosa Parks, whose refusal to give up her seat sparked the Montgomery bus boycott.

Rosa Parks
(February 4, 1913—October 24, 2005)

The woman whose actions ignited the modern day civil rights movement was born Rosa Louise McCauley in Tuskegee, Alabama.

Parks attended Alabama State Teachers College, then she moved to Montgomery with her husband, Raymond Parks.

On December 1, 1955, Parks was arrested for refusing to give up her seat on a bus to a white passenger. The events led to the formation of the Montgomery Improvement Association and the famous bus boycott.

In 2005, Parks passed away at the age of 92. She became the first woman in history to have her casket placed in the rotunda of the United States Capitol, an honor usually reserved for U.S. presidents.

a seamstress. Jim Crow laws required blacks to sit toward the back of public buses. Parks sat in a seat in a middle row. As the bus made its rounds, the front of the bus filled with white people. Then, at one stop, a white person got on board. No seats were available in the front. The man told Parks to move to the back and give him her seat. Parks refused. She was arrested for violating the Jim Crow laws.

Word quickly spread about what had happened, and African Americans were outraged. Several community leaders met to discuss what to do. They formed a group called the Montgomery Improvement Association (MIA). King was asked to lead the group.

The MIA called on all African Americans to boycott, or stop riding, the city buses until the buses stopped segregating blacks and giving preferential treatment to white people. The MIA later filed a lawsuit to overturn Montgomery's segregation laws on buses.

The boycott caused a lot of tension and unhappiness in the community. Most African Americans walked to work or carpooled. Parks and other African Americans lost their jobs because they supported the boycott. The bus companies lost money. A lot of anger was directed at King because he was the MIA's leader. A month after the boycott began, King was arrested on a minor traffic charge. A few days later, a bomb was thrown onto the porch of his home. Mrs. King, one of her friends, and baby Yolanda were inside, but no one was hurt.

The white leaders of Montgomery became desperate to end the boycott. King and other leaders of the MIA were charged with conspiracy to prevent the bus companies from making money. Still, the African-American community continued the protest. In June 1954, a United States Federal District Court ruled that racial segregation on city buses was unconstitutional. The United States Supreme Court later upheld that decision. On December 21, 1956, more than a year after the boycott began, Montgomery buses stopped giving preferential treatment to whites.

"As the days unfolded, I became more and more convinced of the powers of nonviolence," King later wrote. "Nonviolence . . . became a commitment to a way of life."[3] King also called assertive nonviolence "soul force."[4]

The victorious MIA decided to work to overturn all segregation laws. They wanted integration not only in Alabama but everywhere in the United States. In 1957, King and more than one hundred African-American ministers formed a new group to fight against inequality. The group was called the Southern Christian Leadership Conference (SCLC). The SCLC adopted nonviolence to protest unfair laws and practices, and to achieve change. King was elected president of the SCLC.

S.C.L.C.

MARTIN LUTHER KING JR., President
RALPH D. ABERNATHY
VICE-PRESIDENT AT-LARGE
ANDREW J. YOUNG
EXECUTIVE DIRECTOR

FREE & ACCEPTED
MASONS

The headquarters of the Southern Christian Leadership Conference (S.C.L.C.), of which King was elected president, is located in Atlanta, Georgia.

In 1957, Coretta and Martin had their second child, Martin Luther King III. King's first book, *Stride Toward Freedom: The Montgomery Story*, was published in 1958. One day, as he was signing copies of his book in Harlem, New York, a mentally ill African-American woman walked up to him and stabbed him in the chest.[5] King was injured, but he recovered quickly. A year later, King and his wife spent a month in India. King wanted to learn more about Gandhi's nonviolent methods.

By 1960, King was very busy writing, traveling, and speaking. He found it too difficult to lead a congregation by himself because he was so active with the SCLC. King resigned as pastor of Dexter Avenue Baptist Church. He moved with his family to Atlanta, Georgia. He joined his father as co-pastor of Ebenezer Baptist Church. Sharing pastoral duties made it easier for King to devote his time to civil rights.

That same year, on February 1, the first sit-in occurred. A sit-in is a type of protest where demonstrators sit down and refuse to leave a certain place. In this first sit-in, four African-American college students in Greensboro, North Carolina, sat at a segregated lunch counter. They tried to order a meal. The students were denied service, but they refused to leave. Students in other Southern locations began holding sit-ins at restaurants and lunch counters. In October 1960, King participated in a sit-in in Atlanta. He was arrested and charged with violating trespassing laws.

While King continued his work, his wife took care of their growing family. The couple's third child, Dexter, was born in January 1961. Daughter Bernice was born in March 1963. A month after Bernice's birth, King was arrested during a protest in Birmingham, Alabama. He spent several days in jail. During that time, he read a newspaper advertisement sponsored by local white ministers. The ad called King a troublemaker. In response, King wrote a letter to the public on scraps of paper. He explained why he believed it was important to continue to protest peacefully for change. "Letter from a Birmingham Jail" became one of King's most remembered works.

"Oppressed people cannot remain oppressed forever. The yearning for freedom eventually manifests itself, and that is what has happened to the American Negro. Something within has reminded him of his birthright of freedom, and something without has reminded him that it can be gained,"[6] King wrote. ". . . Let us all hope that the dark clouds of racial prejudice will soon pass away and the deep fog of misunderstanding will be lifted from our fear-drenched communities, and in some not too distant tomorrow, the radiant stars of love and brotherhood will shine over our great nation."[7]

King motivated black and white people alike to protest in peace. However, many of the protesters were treated violently. For example, shortly after King was released from the Birmingham jail, schoolchildren in the area planned a protest march. Hundreds gathered at a park near a church and started marching downtown. They linked arms and sang "We Shall Overcome." The young protesters were arrested and put in jail. The next day, more schoolchildren gathered at the park to protest. Birmingham's director of public safety, Eugene "Bull" Connor, ordered the police to attack them with high-powered water hoses and vicious dogs.

In June 1963, President John F. Kennedy sent the bill known as the Civil Rights Act to Congress. King and other leaders of the civil rights movement organized the March on Washington, D.C., for Civil Rights. They wanted to persuade the lawmakers to vote for the bill by showing them how many Americans supported equal rights.

On August 28, 1963, more than two hundred thousand people, black and white, gathered in

King (second from left) and other leaders of the March on Washington pose with President John F. Kennedy in 1963.

Washington, D.C., for the civil rights march. First they went to the Washington Monument. Then they walked to the Lincoln Memorial, where King, the final speaker of the day, delivered his "I have a dream" speech. Earlier that day, King met with President Kennedy, who supported equal rights for all citizens. Later, King was named *Time* magazine's Man of the Year for 1963.

The march was considered a huge success, yet violence continued. Three weeks after the March on Washington, a bomb went off during Sunday school at the Sixteenth Street Baptist Church in Birmingham, Alabama. Four African-American girls were killed. And on November 23, 1963, President Kennedy was shot and killed in Dallas, Texas. His vice president, Lyndon B. Johnson, became president. On July 2, 1964, Johnson signed the Civil Rights Act. This new law ordered desegregation in all public places. It also banned job discrimination based on race.

For his work on behalf of civil rights, King received the Nobel Peace Prize. In December 1964, King traveled with his wife to Oslo, Norway, to accept the honor.

"I accept the Nobel Prize for Peace at a moment when twenty-two million Negroes of the United States are engaged in a creative battle to end the long night of racial injustice," he said. "I accept . . . in behalf of a civil rights movement which is moving with determination and a majestic scorn for risk and danger to establish a reign of freedom and rule of justice."[8]

Despite the passage of the Civil Rights Act, African Americans in the South still faced discrimination. Many were being denied their right to vote. So the demonstrations continued, as did the violence. On several occasions, protesters were

Nobel Prizes

Each year, Nobel Prizes are awarded to people who have made very valuable contributions to the human race. Swedish inventor Alfred Nobel wanted the income from his large estate to be used to fund five annual prizes. The awards are given for the most important discoveries or inventions in physics, chemistry, and physiology; the best literary work; and the most effective work toward international peace. The first award was given in1901.

King displays his Nobel Peace Prize in 1964.

beaten or shot by white police officers or angry white citizens. Some of the protesters died.

"You question—yes, when things happen like this . . . you question sometimes—What are we doing to these people?" King once said.[9]

King himself received death threats. He also was harassed by whites in authority. While he was a hero to many, he was feared and hated by others. "I am tired of demonstrating. I am tired of the threat of death," King once said. "I want to live. I don't want to be a martyr. And there are moments when I doubt if I am going to make it through. . . . I don't march because I want to. I march because I must."[10]

"I can't stop now," King also said. "History has thrust something upon me from which I cannot take away."[11]

In March 1965, thousands of people gathered in Selma, Alabama. They wanted to participate in a protest march to achieve voting rights for African Americans. Three other marches had been attempted. They had all failed. On the first try, protesters were arrested. On the second try, protesters were beaten, and a white minister on the march was killed. On the third attempt, King turned back when the group was confronted by police officers. King wanted to prevent more violence.

On the fourth attempt, President Johnson ordered troopers to guard the peaceful protesters. King led twenty-five thousand people on the march from Selma to Montgomery. When they arrived at the state capital, King gave the governor a petition. Then, he spoke to the crowd.

"We are on the move now," King said. "The burning of our churches will not deter us. We are on the move now. The bombing of our homes will not dissuade us. We are on the move now. The beating and killing of our clergymen and young people will not divert us. . . . We are moving to the land of freedom."[12]

On August 6, 1965, President Johnson signed the Voting Rights Act. Peaceful protest had worked; the legal barrier denying equal rights to African Americans had been removed. However, there was still work to do. Many white people still did not accept blacks as equals.

For the next few years, King continued his mission. He also expanded his concerns. He spoke out against the Vietnam War. He tried to help poor people and those with low-paying jobs.

In April 1968, King traveled to Memphis, Tennessee. African-American sanitation workers had gone on strike. They were protesting unfair work conditions, and King wanted to help.

On April 4, 1968, as he stood on the balcony of the Lorraine Motel, King was shot and killed. His children "were watching television [at home]," his son Dexter King recalled. "That's how I learned. TV told me. . . . We were sitting on the floor watching TV. . . . The Special Bulletin came on, and an unforgettable voice said, 'Dr. Martin Luther King, Jr., has been shot in Memphis, at 6:01 p.m.'"[13]

A white man, former convict James Earl Ray, was arrested. Ray pleaded guilty and was sentenced to ninety-nine years in prison.

The Sunday after King's assassination was declared a day of national mourning. Flags at state buildings were lowered to half mast. King's body was taken to the Georgia Capitol in Atlanta. There, hundreds of thousands of mourners gathered. His funeral was held at Ebenezer Baptist Church. This was the church where King had co-pastored with his father.

While most people mourned King's death peacefully, others did not. News reports told of citizens in Washington, D.C.; Chicago, Illinois; and other communities setting buildings on fire, looting businesses, and threatening police officers. In the years to come, there would be more controversy about how, and even if, Americans should pay official tribute to the fallen civil rights leader.

A huge crowd followed King's casket along the funeral procession route through Atlanta in 1968.

Martin Luther King, Jr., is a hero to many people. These teens take part in a King Day celebration at their school.

Hero for All Americans

Martin Luther King, Jr., inspired many Americans, black and white alike. These citizens did not want King, or his goals, to be forgotten. They believed it was appropriate to honor the civil rights leader with a holiday.

It would not be a holiday just for African Americans, but for all Americans. As King himself once said, "The racial issue that we confront in America is . . . a national problem. Injustice anywhere is a threat to justice everywhere.

Therefore, no American can afford to be apathetic about the problem of racial justice. It's a problem that meets every man at his front door."[1]

"In a very real sense, he was the second father of our country," said Massachusetts senator Edward M. Kennedy, "the second founder of a new world that is not only a place, a piece of geography, but a noble set of ideals."[2]

In April 1968, four days after King was shot, John Conyers introduced a bill in the U.S. House of Representatives to create a federal holiday to honor King. But when the African-American congressman from Michigan submitted the bill, it was a time of great social turmoil in the United States. Even before King's death, many citizens had become discouraged with trying to achieve change through peaceful tactics. They also were angry about the violence that peaceful protesters had endured. They wanted to abandon King's nonviolent tactics. They felt that they had to use force to achieve change.

The Vietnam War (1959–1973) added to the troubles. Many Americans of all ages and races spoke out against the war and staged demonstrations. Some of those demonstrations proved to be deadly. With all the unrest, Congress did not vote on Conyers's bill.

REV. MARTIN LUTHER KING, JR.

1929 — 1968

"Free at last. Free at last.
Thank God Almighty
I'm Free at last."

Martin Luther King, Jr.'s,
tomb reflects in the waters
of the pool that surrounds
it. The tomb is located
on the grounds of the
King Center in Atlanta.

Conyers resubmitted the bill at the next session of Congress. He was joined by Representative Shirley Chisholm of New York. Still, nothing happened at that session, or the next—or for many more sessions after that.

Honoring King was the main focus of his widow, however. Two months after King's death, in June 1968, Coretta Scott King helped to establish the Martin Luther King, Jr. Center for Nonviolent Social Change in Atlanta. It is known as the King Center. The center was founded to preserve King's scholarly work and honors, and to promote his teachings. Mrs. King directed the staff to begin planning a celebration for January 15, 1969. That day would have been her husband's fortieth birthday.

The ceremony featured a church service, speeches, and calls to hold national celebrations of King's birthday in future years. This ceremony became the first of many annual observances held by the center.

Mrs. King wanted to honor her husband on his birthday. She did not want to mark the date he died. Yet in April 1969, several cities held ceremonies to mark the one-year anniversary of King's assassination. Ralph Abernathy became the new leader of the Southern Christian Leadership

Conference (SCLC). On the anniversary of King's death, Abernathy led a march of more than eight thousand blacks and whites through Memphis. They walked from the Lorraine Motel, where King had been killed, to the Memphis City Hall. There, the peaceful demonstrators listened to a speech by Senator Edward Kennedy.

Officials in several cities such as Kansas City, Kansas; Omaha, Nebraska; and Cincinnati, Ohio; declared that April 4, 1969, would be known as Martin Luther King, Jr., Day. Many people called for this day to be named a national holiday.

Richard M. Nixon had been elected president in November 1968. He did not support that idea. Instead, he issued an official statement. The president said he considered the day "a sad anniversary and a somber week . . . a time, no matter what one's race or creed, to rededicate ourselves to the principles of justice and nonviolence for which Dr. King stood."[3]

Riots and acts of violence also were reported on the one-year anniversary of King's death. In Chicago, about four hundred African-American high school students left school. They broke store windows, looted, and threw stones at cars and buses. In a separate incident, white teenagers fired shotguns into a crowd of black teenagers who had gathered outside another high school.[4]

On January 15, 1970, the mayor of Atlanta declared the day to be Martin Luther King, Jr., Day. Approximately one thousand people filled Ebenezer Baptist Church. Among them were Mrs. King and her four children. The crowd sang hymns and heard speeches.

However, schools remained open. Peaceful demonstrators gathered outside the church. Some held signs saying, "New York public schools

Ralph Abernathy (1926–1990)

Ralph Abernathy was born in Linden, Alabama. He earned a B.S. degree from Alabama State College, then went on to Atlanta University where he earned his M.S. degree. In 1948, he became a Baptist minister. Abernathy helped Martin Luther King, Jr., organize bus boycotts to protest racial discrimination in 1955 and 1956.

Abernathy and King helped to form the Southern Christian Leadership Conference (SCLC) in 1957. After King was assassinated, Abernathy became the president of SCLC until 1977. In May 1968, he led a "Poor People's March" on Washington, D.C., which showed the problems faced by those less fortunate.

King served as a co-pastor with his father of the Ebenezer Baptist Church in Atlanta.

closed—Atlanta open—Why?" As *Newsweek* magazine reported, "There was no real pattern and no coordination for the nation's observance of King's birthday."[5]

The SCLC began circulating petitions. These petitions asked Americans to sign their names if they supported a national holiday for King. In April 1971, the SCLC gave Congress petitions that had been signed by 3 million Americans. Still, Congress did not take action.

The last American troops left Vietnam in 1973. That same year, Illinois became the first state to

In 1975, Coretta Scott King gave an interview at the Martin Luther King, Jr. Center for Nonviolent Social Change in Atlanta, Georgia.

adopt King Day. In 1974, Massachusetts and Connecticut established state holidays for King's birthday. That was also the year President Nixon resigned from office because of the Watergate scandal. The vice president, Gerald Ford, became president.

In 1975, the New Jersey State Supreme Court ruled that state workers must receive a paid holiday to honor King. The following year, in November 1976, Jimmy Carter, a former governor of Georgia, defeated Ford in the presidential election.

In November 1978, the National Council of Churches asked Congress to pass a law establishing a holiday for King. Supporters of the King holiday began a new petition campaign.

Mrs. King testified before Congress in February and again in March 1979. She asked the lawmakers to vote in favor of King Day. President Carter voiced his support for the holiday.

Many people did not support honoring King with a holiday. Some of those against the idea were racist. They did not support equal rights, and did not think King deserved a holiday. Others believed that a holiday should honor all who worked for civil rights, not just one individual.

Some people opposing the holiday believed King should be remembered, but not with a national holiday. They thought there were already too many holidays. They also worried that a new federal holiday would be too costly. The government would be required to give overtime pay to federal workers whose jobs required them to work on that day. As one senator once said, "An awful lot of sensible people say we don't need another holiday."[6]

Finally, in November 1979, the House of Representatives voted on the bill to create a holiday for King. The bill was defeated by five votes. It would not go on to the Senate for consideration.

Supporters did not give up. Mrs. King wrote hundreds of letters to local, state, and federal leaders. She asked them to support the bill the next time it was being considered. She also testified before Congress.

In November 1980, Ronald Reagan, a former governor of California, defeated Carter in the presidential election. That same year, Stevie Wonder wrote a song called "Happy Birthday." The popular African-American singer-songwriter was a strong advocate for creating a holiday for King. Wonder wrote the song to gain support for the holiday.

I just never understood

How a man who died for good

Could not have a day that would

Be set aside for his recognition

Because it should never be

Just because some cannot see

The dream as clear as he

That they should make it become
   an illusion

And we all know everything

That he stood for time will bring

For in peace our hearts will sing

Thanks to Martin Luther King[7]

— *"Happy Birthday" by Stevie Wonder*

In 1982, Wonder joined Mrs. King as she presented more petitions supporting the holiday to Tip O'Neill, speaker of the House of Representatives. The next year, on King's birthday, celebrations were held in many cities. They included Los Angeles, California; New York, New York; Baltimore, Maryland; and Seattle, Washington. In Georgia, peaceful demonstrators marched to the state capitol to show their support for a national holiday for King.

President Reagan praised King during his weekly radio address. However, Reagan did not support creating a holiday for the civil rights leader. Reagan felt holidays should be "reserved mainly for the Washingtons and Lincolns," his spokesman said.[8]

Lawmakers continued to debate over the King Day bill. They changed the bill so that the holiday would fall on the third Monday in January. Originally, the bill called for the holiday to be observed on January 15, King's birthday. Some people thought that date was too close to the Christmas and New Year's holidays. The lawmakers changed the bill so that it would have a better chance of passing.

The twentieth anniversary of the March on Washington, D.C., for Civil Rights was in August

1983. That month, the House of Representatives finally voted on a bill to create King Day. Despite the Reagan administration's opposition, the bill passed 338 to 90. The *Boston Globe* published an editorial praising the action. It called the bill "a fitting tribute to an American hero." The newspaper also said the holiday would "keep alive the hope that the dream King had for his own four children—that some day they would be judged not by the color of their skin but by the content of their character—will come true for all children."[9]

The bill next went to the United States Senate for approval. Senator Jesse Helms of North Carolina fought very hard against it. He called King a communist and questioned his personal life. He introduced a bill that said if King deserved a holiday, then so did Hispanic Americans and Thomas Jefferson, among others. Wyoming senator Alan Simpson said Helms turned "an honest debate into something that is divisive, harsh, bitter and manipulative."[10]

Many lawmakers agreed with Simpson. "Dr. King was a healer, and it is in this spirit that I rise," said Senator Robert Dole from Kansas. "It is the belief we commemorate as well as the believer." Senator Charles Mathias from Maryland said, "We

Coretta Scott King and Stevie Wonder are present as President Ronald Reagan signs the King bill into law in 1983.

have waited for more than a century since the end of the Civil War for this moment of reconciliation."[11]

In the end, Helms lost. In October 1983, the Senate voted 78 to 22 in favor of the King Day bill. Mrs. King, Wonder, and others sat in the Senate gallery as the bill was approved. "For those of us who believe in the dream, it is a great day for America and the world," Mrs. King said. "We are proud to be Americans, but today we are even prouder."[12]

The bill next went to President Reagan for signature. Reagan had not supported a national holiday for King. He had received a petition from the Conservative Caucus asking him to veto the bill. The petition had been signed by more than forty-three thousand people. Many people worried that Reagan would not sign the bill, but Reagan changed his mind.

On November 3, 1983, Coretta Scott King stood with family members in the Rose Garden of the White House. She was joined by Wonder, leaders of the civil rights movement, government officials, and other important people. The group had gathered to witness the president sign the King bill into law. Starting in 1986, the third Monday of every January would be a holiday to honor Martin

Coretta Scott King
(April 27, 1927—January 30, 2006)

Born and raised in Heiberger, Alabama, Coretta Scott became familiar with the hardships of discrimination and segregation at an early age.

While in college in Boston, she met Martin Luther King, Jr. The couple married on June 15, 1953, and in 1954 moved to Montgomery, Alabama.

After her husband's death, Mrs. King focused on continuing his work by building The Martin Luther King, Jr.

Center for Nonviolent Social Change, also called The King Center. It opened to the public in 1981.

After turning over leadership of the King Center to her son Dexter in 1995, she continued to be active in causes such as AIDS education and curbing gun violence, among others, until her death at age 78 in 2006.

Coretta Scott King speaks at an observance of King Day at Oklahoma State University in 2005.

Luther King, Jr. Federal workers would get the day off with pay.

"The man whose words and deeds stirred our nation to the very depths of its soul was Dr. Martin Luther King, Jr.," the president said. "In a nation that proclaimed liberty and justice for all, too many black Americans were living with neither."[13]

The president also said, "Traces of bigotry still mar America. So each year on Martin Luther King Day, let us not only recall Dr. King but rededicate ourselves to the commandments he believed in and sought to live each day: 'Thou shalt love thy God with all thy heart and thou shall love thy neighbor as thyself.'"[14]

Mrs. King had worked very hard and for a very long time to make the holiday a reality. She also spoke during the bill-signing ceremony. "All right-thinking people . . . are joined in spirit with us this day as the highest recognition this nation gives is bestowed on Martin Luther King, Jr.," she said. "America is a more democratic nation. America is a more just nation. America is a more peaceful nation because Martin Luther King, Jr. became her preeminent nonviolent commander."[15]

In 2005, residents of a town in Ohio march downtown in celebration of Martin Luther King, Jr., Day.

Celebrating,
State by State

I t was a cold and rainy Friday in January, 2005, but the weather did not dampen the spirits of many students at Weyanoke Elementary School in Alexandria, Virginia. They had a lively activity planned for that day: a peaceful protest through the school's hallways to voice their concerns about environmental issues affecting the nation's deserts.

The second-grade students were combining what they had learned about the environment with what they had learned about Dr. Martin Luther King, Jr. They had learned that King supported nonviolence to achieve equal rights. They learned he had become known throughout the world for working peacefully to achieve change. The students learned about the March on Washington D.C., for Civil Rights. They listened to King's famous "I have a dream" speech.

With the help of their teachers, the students organized the protest march. Carrying signs and chanting, "Save our deserts!" and other slogans, the students marched through the hallways of Weyanoke. They proceeded to the fifth-grade classrooms. There, they peacefully—though noisily—continued their protest.

"They made a peaceful protest to make people aware of the [desert] problem," recalled Haban, a fifth-grader at Weyanoke.[1] Said his classmate Nathaniel, "Just like Dr. King fought [peacefully] for what he believed in, the second graders fought for what they believed in. I think they [the second-grade students] did an excellent job."[2]

"When you protest, you're fighting for what you think is right, and needed," said Marvin, another fifth-grader at Weyanoke. The second-graders protested for what was right, and needed, he said, and "so did Martin Luther King Jr."[3]

The Weyanoke students' protest march was to celebrate King Day. Back in November 1983, President Reagan had signed the bill establishing a federal holiday for the fallen civil rights leader. The bill stated that starting in 1986, the third Monday of every January would be designated as the holiday. Federal workers would get the day off with pay.

However, this bill did not require the fifty states to recognize King Day as a holiday for their own workers or schoolchildren. Each state would have to adopt the holiday on its own. In August 1984, Reagan signed a bill that established the Martin Luther King, Jr., Federal Holiday Commission. The goal of the commission was to persuade all fifty states to adopt King Day.

The commission was given five years to complete its work. After that time, the commission could receive an extension of another five years. The commission met for the first time in November 1984. The group elected Coretta Scott King as chairperson.

On January 20, 1986, the first national King Day was observed. Already, seventeen states had official King holidays. Some states modified the holiday. For example, Virginia included celebrations for Confederate generals Robert E. Lee and

Some supporters in San Francisco, California, celebrate Martin Luther King, Jr., Day with a march downtown.

Stonewall Jackson on King Day. Utah called King Day Human Rights Day.

Some states resisted adopting the holiday. Arizona was one such state. Lawmakers introduced several resolutions, or bills, to honor King, but each one failed to gain enough support. In May 1986, another bill to honor King failed. Arizona governor Bruce Babbitt then signed an executive order authorizing the holiday. The following month, the Arizona attorney general ruled that the governor did not have the power to declare a legal holiday. In January 1987, the new governor, Evan Mecham, rescinded Babbitt's order.

Inspired by King's call to protest peacefully for social change, King Day supporters called for a tourism boycott of Arizona. When tourists visit a state, they spend money on hotels, food, souvenirs, and other items. Their spending helps the economy of the state they are visiting. The Montgomery, Alabama, bus boycott during the 1950s hurt that city's economy and brought an end to segregation on buses.

King Day supporters in Arizona hoped a tourism boycott would hurt Arizona's economy so much that state lawmakers would be persuaded to change their minds and vote to support a state holiday to honor King.

"We met with Governor Mecham and asked him please, please don't do it [rescind the order]," said Warren Stewart, a minister in Phoenix who led a boycott group called Victory Now. "But we didn't support a national boycott until that March." That was when several more bills to honor King were introduced by Arizona lawmakers. They all failed, too. "We lobbied the legislature to enact the holiday," Stewart said, "and they turned up their noses at us."[4]

Mecham issued a proclamation in June 1987. It declared the third Sunday in January Martin Luther King, Jr.—Civil Rights Day in Arizona. It was a compromise, but King holiday backers were not happy. They stepped up boycott efforts. Several national groups that had planned meetings or conventions in Arizona canceled.

Reagan served as president until 1988. His vice president, George H.W. Bush, was elected president in 1988. By 1989, King Day had been adopted in forty-four of the fifty states. Arizona remained one of the holdouts. In September 1989, the Arizona Legislature passed a bill that created a paid state holiday to honor King. At the same time, the bill eliminated Columbus Day as a paid state holiday. Many citizens did not like that. They gathered enough signatures on petitions to call for a vote. The citizens' votes would determine the solution to the issue.

In November 1990, Arizona citizens went to the polls. They could vote for either Proposition 301 or Proposition 302. Proposition 301 would have created a King holiday and eliminated Columbus Day. It was overwhelmingly rejected. Proposition

Marchers make their way up a street in Seattle, Washington, during a King Day parade.

302 would have added the King celebration and brought back Columbus Day. This proposition lost, too, by less than one percent of the vote.[5]

The boycott went into high gear. Several more groups canceled plans to travel to Arizona. In 1991, the National Football League moved the Super Bowl from Arizona to California to honor the boycott. Arizona officials estimate they lost almost $200 million in tourism dollars because of the boycott.[6]

Finally, in November 1992, Arizona citizens voted again on whether to establish a King Day. This time, the bill passed. That state's holiday is called Martin Luther King, Jr./Civil Rights Day. Each year, it is observed on the third Monday in January. Arizona's first official holiday was on January 18, 1993.

Bush served one term as president. He was defeated in the November 1992 presidential election by Bill Clinton, a former governor of Arkansas. In August 1994, President Clinton signed the Martin Luther King, Jr., Federal Holiday and Service Act. This act stated that the goal of King Day was for citizens to serve the community, and work toward peace and justice. Clinton also extended the King commission for five years.

In 1995, however, the commission voted to disband. The Clinton administration had been cutting some government programs to balance the federal budget. The commission decided to break up to save taxpayer money. The commission turned its duties over to the King Center. This center was founded by Mrs. King to ensure her husband's message lived on.

Some people worried that with the commission gone, states might turn their back on King Day. "As long as it's seen as a federal mandate, states are willing to support the effort," said Phillip Caldwell, chairman of the King holiday commission in Montana. "But in states like Montana, where the [African-American] population is less than 10 percent, I think [the effort] will have a very difficult time obtaining any kind of funding or support."[7]

Caldwell need not have worried. In 1999, New Hampshire became the last state to officially recognize King Day. State lawmakers changed the name of Civil Rights Day to King Day.

Today, all fifty states recognize the holiday to honor Martin Luther King, Jr. Every year, on the third Monday in January, federal and state offices, banks, and public schools close for King Day. Children in many private schools also enjoy the day off. So do some people who work for privately owned companies. These businesses are not required by law to honor the holiday. In 1998, the Bureau of National Affairs conducted a study. It asked 458 employers if they gave their workers a paid day off for King Day. The study found that 26 percent did, indeed, give employees a paid day off for King Day.[8]

Martin Luther King III applauds as Governor Jeanne Shaheen of New Hampshire signs the bill in 1999 that finally recognizes Martin Luther King, Jr., Day as a holiday in her state.

King was not a hero just for Americans. He was an international role model as well. During his lifetime, he traveled to Africa and India, among other countries, and was awarded the Nobel Peace Prize. After he died, Mrs. King continued to deliver her husband's message. She participated in protests, and made goodwill trips to Latin America, Europe, and Asia, among other places.

It is no wonder, then, that Americans are not the only people who mark King Day. In the African country of Cameroon, a ceremony was held during one King Day to celebrate the completion of a community water project. According to the King Center, more than one hundred other nations mark King Day with celebrations in honor of the civil rights leader.

A student kneels to find out more information about Martin Luther King, Jr., at a college in New Mexico.

5

Remember! Celebrate! Act!

Unlike many holidays, there are no symbols associated with King Day. However, the holiday does have an official theme. It is, "Remember! Celebrate! Act! A day on, not a day off." This means remembering Martin Luther King, Jr., and what he worked for, and thinking about ways people can make a positive difference in their own communities. It means celebrating King's life with concerts, musical performances, educational programs, art shows, and readings of his works.

It also means completing community service and volunteer projects. Unlike many holidays, King Day is not a day to receive gifts. Instead, it is a day to give gifts—the gifts of time, effort, and love. The holiday is not supposed to be just another day off from school or work, a chance to hang out with friends or go shopping. It is a day to be "on," to be doing things to make the world a better place.

"We commemorate . . . the man of action, who put his life on the line for freedom and justice every day," his widow, Coretta Scott King, once wrote. "We commemorate [the] great dream of a vibrant, multiracial nation united in justice, peace and reconciliation."[1]

King Day is "above all a day of service," Mrs. King wrote. ". . . It is a day of volunteering to feed the hungry, rehabilitate housing, tutoring . . . mentoring . . . consoling the broken-hearted and a thousand other projects for building the beloved community of his dream."[2]

King Day celebrations usually include acts of service, such as giving blood and helping the needy. They also include speeches by civil rights leaders. Some King Day celebrations include peaceful protests, such as the Weyanoke Elementary School march to save the desert.

On King Day 2000, thousands of people protested at the state capital in South Carolina. They wanted lawmakers to remove the Confederate battle flag that was flying there.

"This is the kind of thing we need to be doing on Martin Luther King's birthday," said his eldest son, Martin Luther King III. "The flag is a terrible symbol that brings a lot of negative energy. And while we believe the [Confederate] flag has an appropriate place, it just does not belong on top of the Capitol because it is not a sign of unification."[3]

During King Day 2005 celebrations, citizens in Gallup, New Mexico, held a unity march. In Oakland, California, people attended a peace celebration and rally. The city of Dallas, Texas, threw a King Day parade. Kids of all ages in Asheville, North Carolina, attended a youth celebration. Young and old alike marched on a freedom walk in Bemidji, Minnesota. The community of Mesa, Arizona, held a night of tribute.

The 2005 King Day celebrations were particularly poignant. Less than a month earlier, on December 26, 2004, a powerful undersea earthquake erupted. It set off a tsunami, which is a series of huge waves. The tsunami traveled across the Indian Ocean. Approximately three hundred thousand people in Asia and Africa died.

Hundreds of thousands of others lost their homes and jobs.

Meanwhile, American soldiers were still fighting in Afghanistan and Iraq. On King Day 2005, many American citizens took time to reflect on the international turmoil. Near Denver, Colorado, citizens gathered at a restaurant and bar called Brother Jeff's Cultural Caf. "The message [for King Day] every year is powerful, but it's heightened this year because of what is going on in the world . . . " said one person who was there. "It doesn't take away from Dr. King and his message, to be the best you can be, everybody makes a difference, everybody is powerful in their own way."[4]

Other King Day celebrations that year focused on local problems, such as school shootings. In Denver, approximately six thousand people participated in a two-mile "marade," a march and a parade. It was believed to be one of America's largest annual parades for King Day.

King "wanted America to live up to its promise," said one marcher, who was joined by his wife and four children. "When we were separate, we were not equal. He fought for equality."[5]

In California, Governor Arnold Schwarzenegger's wife, Maria Shriver, helped pack food

Mohandas Karamchand Gandhi
(October 2, 1869—January 30, 1948)

Born on October 2, 1869, in Porbandar, India, Gandhi would become one of the greatest spiritual, political, moral, and cultural leaders of the twentieth century. Known as the Mahatma, or Great Soul, the people of India honor Gandhi as the father of their nation.

In 1947, India was granted its independence from Britain. Gandhi was upset by the split of the country into India and Pakistan, and by the fighting between Hindus and Muslims. Gandhi began his final fast on January 13, 1948, at the age of 78. His fast lasted five days before leaders of Hindu, Muslim, and other groups agreed to stop the bloodshed. On January 30, while on the way to a prayer meeting, Gandhi was assassinated.

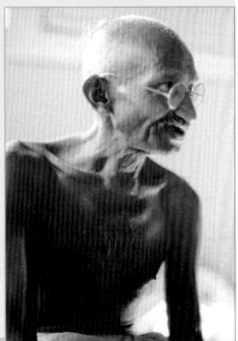

Gandhi is shown here in an undated photograph one hour after his release from a government prison in India.

boxes at the Community Action Partnership of Orange County. The boxes of nonperishable goods were distributed to needy families and senior citizens in Orange County.

"I thank each and every one of you," Shriver told the other volunteers. "You could have been at the beach, at a playground or just hanging around. But you made a choice to come here and help other people. . . . You are my heroes."[6]

Shriver also talked about Mahatma Gandhi. Gandhi was the Indian leader whose nonviolent acts achieved social change for his country. Gandhi had been a great influence on King. Shriver quoted Gandhi, who once said, "The best way to find yourself is to lose yourself in service."[7]

Students in Providence–St. Mel School in Chicago celebrated King Day 2005 in an unusual way: They actually went to school. The day started with an assembly. It featured a reading of King's six principles of nonviolence. Those principles are to accept nonviolence as a way of life; try to gain understanding through nonviolence; work against injustice; believe that suffering educates and transforms; choose love over hate; and believe that the universe is on the side of justice.[8]

The students also heard musical performances. Then, they went to their classrooms. The

Thousands of people take part in the annual "marade" in Denver, which is believed to be one of the largest annual parades for King.

younger students performed a play about Rosa Parks and the bus boycott in Montgomery, Alabama. The older students discussed how communities throughout the world can practice nonviolence to achieve change.

"It's always good to go to school to learn more about what happened in the past," said one eighth-grader. "I feel that Dr. King would want us to be in school on his birthday because this is what he strived for, for us to be together as a group and not segregated."[9]

Another student said that King "went through a lot for us to be here right now. That's why it's important for us to be in school today, to learn more about the civil rights struggle."[10]

Older students also marked King Day 2005 in meaningful ways. College students at Tulane University in New Orleans, Louisiana, sponsored a workshop for the residents of Odyssey House. Odyssey House is a live-in program for people fighting drug addiction. The workshop sessions focused on diet, exercise, health, and serving as positive role models for young people.

The event organizer said the workshop was a success. It not only helped the residents of Odyssey House, but it also fulfilled the mission of King Day. "It really covered our purpose of a

Volunteers help to clean up at Mary Bethune Middle School for homeless children in West Long Beach, California, in honor of Martin Luther King, Jr., Day.

day on, versus a day off," the organizer said. "I wish that everyone, in all groups . . . will also use [King Day] for service activities."[11]

In Washington, D.C., several volunteers helped to repaint Roosevelt Senior High School. Most of the school's population is African American. Most of the volunteers were white.

"I said to myself, this is what he was about— bringing people of different races together at one time for one common vision," said one teen who is a student at Roosevelt. "This is his legacy in action."[12]

In Bethesda, Maryland, near Washington, D.C., families from several churches gathered with elected officials at a hotel conference room. They listened to speakers. Then they participated in service projects. They made greeting cards for service members in Iraq. They also made cards for service members at Walter Reed Army Medical Center who were recovering from war injuries. The conference attendees also decorated place mats for their local Meals on Wheels program.

Elsewhere near the nation's capital, more than one hundred students and adults performed at the eleventh annual King Festival in Chantilly, Virginia. The students produced the event. "I know if it weren't for Dr. King I wouldn't be able to live in the neighborhood where I live; I wouldn't attend the school I go to," said one teen who wrote and performed three songs. "Basically, I wouldn't be able to have this life."[13]

King "challenged all of us . . . not only to live up to the ideals upon which this nation was founded but also to . . . make the ideal of justice and equality something more than words," wrote Jill Nelson online as part of AOL Black Voices. Nelson also wrote that she would spend King Day reading King's works.

"Libraries are full of books by and about King—for adults and children," she said. "Each of us should spend part of that day not only reminding ourselves of the principles for which he lived and died but also contemplating how we can make them real."[14]

Christina Mathis is one example of how King's dreams of a better society are being realized. The twenty-one year old from California has dedicated much of her life to helping others. She learned about King through her mother. When Mathis was a child, her mother taught her King's "I have a dream" speech. Mathis memorized it. She performed it for churches in her community.

Later, Mathis joined the California Conservation Corps. This program offers college scholarships and credits to those who work on environmental service projects. Mathis also participates in other community service projects. She helps others not only on King Day but throughout the year.

"For Dr. King's birthday [in 2005], I'll be serving food to homeless people at a shelter," Mathis wrote in *Parade* magazine. "Last Thanksgiving, I helped feed over 400 people. It touched my heart, because families came in with their children . . . and just putting warm food on their plates made me feel good."[15]

"There's always someone who has less than I do," she added. "We were embracing those kids and letting them know things would get better. Dr. King had hope, and I share his hope."[16]

The year 2006 marked the twentieth anniversary of the federal holiday honoring King. In Lima, Ohio, several activities were planned. They included a concert featuring gospel singer CeCe Winans, a breakfast to honor schoolchildren who participated in an essay contest, a freedom march, and lectures.

Some people remembered the victims of Hurricane Katrina in their holiday observances. In that huge natural disaster of late August 2005, parts of Louisiana, Mississippi, and Alabama were devastated. The city of New Orleans in Louisiana was hit particularly hard when the levees protecting the city from Lake Pontchartrain were breached, causing severe flooding.

In all, Hurricane Katrina caused approximately $75 billion in damages, and killed well more than a thousand people. (As of early 2006, final figures were not yet known because so many people were still unaccounted for.) In New Orleans, the majority of those most severely affected by the hurricane were poor Americans who did not have the resources to evacuate the city.

"In King's time, the oppression of some was based on an obvious difference, the color of one's skin. But today the problem is much more subtle," wrote Virginia Tech college student Brandon Guichard for the online resource *University Wire*. "Recall the heartbreaking images from New Orleans. . . . The tragic reality is that too many of our fellow citizens are being excluded by poverty."[17]

House Democratic leader Nancy Pelosi said, ". . . On this day and every day, it is not enough simply to remember his ideals and his many accomplishments. We must adopt them and continue them. We must make them our own."[18]

The civil rights leader has been gone a long time, but he is not forgotten. Through the holiday named in his honor, King's good intentions live on.

People line the streets in Los Angeles, California, during a parade to honor Martin Luther King, Jr.

The Legacy
Lives On

All over the United States, streets and schools are named after Martin Luther King, Jr. He has received many other honors. Soon, he will be the recipient of a very high honor: A memorial to King will be built on the National Mall in Washington, D.C.

A private group called the Martin Luther King, Jr., National Memorial Project Foundation raised money to build the memorial. The group announced in January 2005 that it had raised about one-third of the $100 million needed. Construction is scheduled to begin in 2006.

The National Mall is a space reserved to honor America's most important historical figures. The King memorial will be the first on the mall to honor an African American. "King did as much for this country as many presidents did," said Washington, D.C., delegate Eleanor Holmes. "The Mall is where he belongs."[1]

The Lorraine Motel in Memphis, Tennessee, was once associated with the tragedy of King's assassination. Now, it is an educational tool. It is also a reminder of the bravery and dedication of others. When King was killed, the motel was owned by an African-American businessman. The motel struggled financially after King's assassination in 1968. By 1982, it had gone out of business.

A group of investors decided to pool their resources and save the motel as an important historic site. They raised money to turn the motel into the National Civil Rights Museum. The museum opened in September 1991. Its exhibits tell the story of the civil rights movement.

King's message has also been spread by the Martin Luther King, Jr. Center for Nonviolent Social Change in Atlanta, Georgia. Coretta Scott King, widow of the civil rights leader, founded the

Exhibits at the National Civil Rights Museum in Memphis, Tennessee, tell the story of the Civil Rights Movement.

center more than thirty-five years ago. It is the first institution built to honor an African-American leader.

The King Center has inspired and motivated many people, individuals as well as large corporations. In December 2003, the Denny's restaurant chain announced that it would ask people to commit to community service to honor King.

Denny's also pledged to raise $1 million to help the King Center create a program on service learning. The program is distributed to hundreds of youth groups in the United States. In a press release, Denny's said community service is important because so many nonprofit groups rely on unpaid volunteers.

"Denny's is helping us realize [King's] dream . . . for America by teaching the critical importance of service and how it can mold and build a local community," Mrs. King once said. She added that her husband's dream "was to make community service a way of life, not just a single day of service that we celebrate . . . on his birthday."[2]

The King Center offers programs and services on racism, bigotry, and discrimination. It also focuses on the problems of child poverty, acquired immune deficiency syndrome (AIDS), domestic and international violence, and fewer educational opportunities for some Americans, among other topics.

The center is part of a twenty-three acre national park. The site includes the house where King was born in 1929. More than one million people visit the site each year. That makes it the most visited cultural and tourist attraction in the southeastern United States.

Until 1995, Mrs. King was the founding president, chair, and chief executive officer of the King Center. Then, her son Dexter King took over. He served as chairman, president, and chief executive officer until January 2004. At that time, eldest son Martin Luther King III became president and chief executive officer. Mrs. King was named interim chair until 1995, when Dexter King took over her duties.

When her husband was killed in 1968, Mrs. King was left with four young children to raise on her own. She devoted the rest of her life to raising her family and making sure her husband's legacy would live on.

"People asked me how I was able to do this and raise four children at the same time," she said in 1999. "I can only reply that when God calls you to a great task, he provides you with the strength to accomplish what he has called you to do."[3]

Mrs. King had a heart attack and a stroke in the summer of 2005. She was unable to speak or walk, yet she maintained her sense of purpose. In January 2006, Mrs. King attended the Salute to Greatness banquet. The annual banquet is part of the King Center's holiday celebration, and it raises money for the center and its programs.

On January 30, 2006, Mrs. King died in her sleep. She was 78 years old. Flags at the Capitol in Washington, D.C., were lowered to half-mast to honor her. Dignitaries and celebrities all over the world praised her.

"She carried on the legacy of her husband . . . including through her extraordinary work at the King Center," said President George W. Bush. "Mrs. King's lasting contributions to freedom and equality have made America a better and more compassionate nation."[4]

Said Thabo Mbeki, the president of South Africa, "Like all great champions, she learned to function with pain and keep serving. So her legacy is secure as a freedom fighter, but her work remains unfinished."[5]

With Mrs. King's passing, there are questions about what will happen next with the King Center. The building itself needs several million dollars worth of renovations. Two of the King children, Dexter and Yolanda, are in favor of selling the center to the National Park Service. So are other board members of the center, including former United Nations ambassador Andrew Young and Christine King Farris, sister of Martin Luther King, Jr. However, two of the King children, Martin III and Bernice, are against the sale. They want to keep the center as a family-run operation.[6]

Who will operate the center may be unknown at this time. But through King Day, the legacy of the civil rights leader lives on. Remember. Act. Celebrate.

On the King Center web site, Mrs. King once wrote a piece encouraging all Americans to celebrate every King Day in the manner in which the holiday was intended. She noted that her husband once said, "We all have to decide whether we 'will walk in the light of creative altruism or the darkness of destructive selfishness.' Life's most persistent . . . question, he said, is 'what are you doing for others?'"[7]

So what are you doing for others? And how will you celebrate on King Day?

Get Active in Your Own Community

1 One of the goals of King Day is for people to give their time, effort, and love to make their community a better place. What better way to do that than to take on a service project?

2 A service project is an organized activity to benefit someone else. It can be something as simple as joining with friends to pick up trash from the school playground, volunteering to help younger students in math or spelling, or asking for donations of canned goods to help neighbors in need.

3 Get your entire family involved to live out the ideals of Martin Luther King, Jr. And remember: Service projects make the biggest difference when they are a year-round activity, and not just something to do on King Day.

advocate—Someone who supports the cause of another.

assassination—The killing of someone well known; usually done secretly.

bigotry—Unwillingness to accept people of a different race or religion.

boycott—Refusing to have dealings with something; used to express disapproval or to force the acceptance of certain conditions.

demonstration—A public display of group feelings toward a person or cause.

disband—To break up an organization.

discriminate—To make a difference in treatment or favor for some reason other than individual merit.

goodwill—Approval, support.

integrate—To bring into equal membership in society or an organization.

just—Reasonable, proper.

legislation—Rules or laws approved by an official group.

manifest—To make evident or certain by showing or displaying.

martyr—Person who sacrifices something of great value, especially life, for a belief.

minstrel—Type of musical entertainer in the 19th century.

oppression—Unjust or cruel use of authority or power.

petition—Formal written request made to an official person or group.

prejudice—Negative opinion formed without facts or information.

protest—Complaint, objection, or display of unwillingness, usually directed to an idea or course of action.

racism—Belief that heritage determines abilities and value, and that some heritages are less able and valuable than others.

segregation—Policy of separating people by race.

sit-in—Type of protest where people sit down and refuse to leave.

somber—Dark and gloomy.

transport—To take from one place to another.

Tsunami—Series of huge waves.

CHAPTER NOTES

◆ Chapter 1. ". . . A Dream Today!"

1. Juan Williams, "A Dream Remembered," *New York Times*, August 28, 1003, p. A-31.
2. Ibid.
3. Gay Talese, "A Happy Day in Harlem: Bar Patron's 'I Wish I Was There' Tells Feeling of Many Watching Rally on TV," *New York Times*, August 29, 1963, p. A-19.
4. James Reston, "'I Have a Dream . . .': Peroration by Dr. King Sums Up A Day the Capital Will Remember," *New York Times*, August 29, 1963, p. A-1.
5. Martin Luther King, Jr., *I Have a Dream: Writings and Speeches That Changed the World*, edited by James M. Washington (San Francisco: Harper, 1992), p. 104.
6. Reston.
7. Ibid.

◆ Chapter 2. Leader of the Movement

1. Biography Resource Center: Martin Luther King Jr., Fairfax County, Virginia, Public

Library Web site, n.d., <www.co.fairfax.va.us/library> (January 18, 2005).

2. Patricia McKissack and Fredrick McKissack, *Martin Luther King, Jr., Man of Peace* (Springfield, New Jersey: Enslow Publishers, 1991), p. 11.

3. Martin Luther King, Jr., *I Have a Dream: Writings and Speeches That Changed the World*, edited by James M. Washington (San Francisco: Harper, 1992), p. 159.

4. Stewart Burns, *To the Mountaintop: Martin Luther King, Jr.'s Sacred Mission to Save America 1955–1968* (New York: Harper-Collins Publishers, 2004), p. 457.

5. Biography Resource Center.

6. Martin Luther King, Jr., *Why We Can't Wait* (New York: Penguin Books, 1964), p. 91.

7. Ibid., p. 100.

8. King, edited by Washington, p. 108.

9. Marshall Frady, *Martin Luther King, Jr.* (New York: Viking, Penguin Books, 2002), p. 8.

10. Ibid., pp. 189–190.

11. Ibid., p. 53.

12. King, edited by Washington, p. 122.

13. Dexter Scott King with Ralph Wiley, *Growing Up King* (New York: Warner Books, 2003), p. 47.

◆ Chapter 3. Hero for All Americans

1. Martin Luther King, Jr., *I Have a Dream: Writings and Speeches That Changed the World*, edited by James M. Washington (San Francisco: Harper, 1992), p. 67.

2. David Rogers, "Senate OKs Holiday to Honor King," *Boston Globe*, October 20, 1983, p. A-1.

3. "A Dream—Still Unfulfilled," *Newsweek*, April 16, 1969, pp. 34–35.

4. Ibid.

5. "Anniversaries: King Day," *Newsweek*, January 26, 1970, p. 24.

6. David M. Alpern with Gloria Borger, "Behind the King Debate," *Newsweek*, October 31, 1983, p. 32.

7. Stevie Wonder lyrics to "Happy Birthday," as posted on <http://www.seeklyrics.com/lyrics/Stevie-Wonder/Happy-Birthday.html> (March 15, 2006).

8. Associated Press, "King Lauded in Speeches Across U.S.; Call for a National Holiday," *Boston Globe*, January 16, 1983. p. A-1.

9. "Martin Luther King and America," *Boston Globe*, August 5, 1983, p. A-1.

10. Alpern with Borger.

11. Rogers.

12. Ibid.

13. Associated Press, "Reagan Signs Bill—King Holiday Official," *Boston Globe*, November 2, 1983, p. A-1.

14. Michael Eric Dyson, *I May Not Get There with You: The True Martin Luther King, Jr.* (New York: The Free Press, a Division of Simon & Schuster, 2000), p. 225.

15. Associated Press, November 2, 1983.

◆ Chapter 4. Celebrating, State by State

1. Student papers at Weyanoke Elementary School, Alexandria, Virginia, collected for author by Mrs. Linda Dunn, second-grade teacher at Weyanoke; January 2005.

2. Ibid.

3. Ibid.

4. Alan Gottlieb, "1987–1982 Boycott of Arizona may offer lessons to Colorado," *Denver Post*, January 17, 1993.

5. Ibid.

6. "Migrant legislation draws all for Arizona boycott," *Arizona Republic*, March 24, 2005.

7. "MLK Federal Holiday Commission Votes to Disband," Jet, June 19, 1995, p. 21.

8. "The King Holiday: A Chronology," n.d., <http://www.thekingcenter.org/holiday/kho_chronology.html> (March 15, 2006).

◆ Chapter 5. **Remember! Celebrate! Act!**

1. Coretta Scott King, "The Meaning of the Martin Luther King, Jr. Holiday," n.d., <http://www.thekingcenter.org/holiday/index.asp.> (March 15, 2006).

2. Ibid.

3. "Thousands march against Confederate flag in South Carolina," CNN.com, January 17, 2000, <http://transcripts.cnn.com/2000/ALLPOLITICS/stories/01/17/sc.flag/> (March 15, 2006).

4. Elizabeth Aguilera, "'A celebration of how far we've come': Thousands gather to march in honor of slain civil rights leader Martin Luther King Jr." *Denver Post*, January 18, 2005, p. B-1.

5. Ibid.

6. David Reyes, "Shriver Uses Holiday to Dig In and Help Out; The first lady urges volunteers in Garden Grove to keep up the good works beyond King day," *Los Angeles Times*, January 18, 2005, p. B-5.

7. Ibid.

8. Anne Schraff, *Coretta Scott King: Striving for Civil Rights* (Springfield, New Jersey: Enslow Publishers, 1997), pp. 100–101.

9. Karen Pride, "Students honor King by staying in school," *Chicago Defender,* Vol. XCIX, Iss. 180 January 18, 2005, p. 2.

10. Ibid.

11. T. Phillip Washington, "King Day used as day 'on,' not 'off'; Odyssey House gets a message of hope," *Times-Picayune*, January 30, 2005, p. 1.

12. Vanessa Williams, "Living Out the Dream In Memory of King; Area Events Offer Activities Centered on Civil Rights Leader's Ideals," *Washington Post*, January 18, 2005, p. B-1.

13. Matthew Perrone, "MLK Day: Much more than a Day Off," n.d., <http://www.times community.com/site/tab5.cfm?newsid= 13737832&BRD=2553&PAG=461&dept_id =511686&rfi=6> (January 18, 2005).

14. Jill Nelson, "What Should You Do on MLK Day?" NiaOnline, AOLBlack Voices, January 17, 2005, <http://blackvoices. aol.com/mlk/observingarticle> (March 15, 2006).

15. Paula Silverman, "Fresh Voices: I Dedicate My Service to Dr. King," *Parade*, January 16, 2005, p. 18.

16. Ibid.

17. Brandon Guichard, "Much left to be done to achieve King's dream of equality," copyright Financial Times Ltd., from University Wire, distributed January 18, 2006.

18. Ellen Simon, "Pelosi: 'As Our Nation Celebrates Martin Luther King Day, We Remember His Vision for an America of Opportunity and Equality,'" copyright Financial Times Ltd., from U.S. Newswire, distributed January 13, 2006.

◆ Chapter 6. The Legacy Lives On

1. Theola S. Labbe, "Memorial to King Drives On; Mall Project Raises a Third of Funds," *Washington Post*, January 16, 2005, p. C-1.

2. King Center Press Release: "Denny's Presents New Year's Resolution Challenge—Make a Difference in our Local Community."

3. Michelle Hiskey, "An Abiding Love: Wedded to the cause, 'My wife was always stronger than I was through the struggle,'" *Atlanta Journal and Constitution*, February 7, 2006, Special Section.

4. "Thoughts on Coretta," *Philadelphia Daily News*, via Knight-Ridder/Tribune Business News, February 1, 2006.

5. Ibid.

6. Errin Haines, "Family feud, new book threaten to distract from King's legacy," copyright Financial Times Ltd., from AP Worldstream, January 15, 2006.

7. Coretta Scott King, "The Meaning of the Martin Luther King, Jr. Holiday," *The King Center*, n.d., <http://thekingcenter.com/holiday/index.asp> (January 15, 2006).

FURTHER READING

Books

Farris, Christine King. *My Brother Martin: A Sister Remembers Growing Up With the Rev. Dr. Martin Luther King Jr.* New York: Simon & Schuster Books for Young Readers, 2003.

Giovanni, Nikki. *Rosa.* New York: Henry Holt, 2005.

Gogerly, Liz. *The Dream of Martin Luther King.* Austin, Tex.: Raintree Steck-Vaughn Publishers, 2004.

Hatt, Christine. *Martin Luther King, Jr.* Milwaukee, Wisc.: World Almanac Library, 2004.

Levine, Michelle. *Rosa Parks.* Minneapolis, Minn.: Compass Point, 2005.

Mcwhorter, Diane. *A Dream of Freedom: The Civil Rights Movement from 1954 to 1968.* New York: Scholastic, 2004.

Murcia, Rebecca Thatcher. *The Civil Rights Movement.* Hockessin, Del.: Mitchell Lane, 2005.

Pinkney, Andrea Davis. *Let it Shine: Stories of Black Women Freedom Fighters.* San Diego, Calif.: Harcourt, 2000.

INTERNET ADDRESSES

Martin Luther King, Jr.: Day of Service
<http://www.mlkday.org>

Find out what you can do in your community for Martin Luther King, Jr., Day.

Time 100: Martin Luther King, Jr.
<http://www.time.com/time/time100/leaders/ profile/king.html>

Learn about King's impact as a leader.

INDEX